HERITAGE TRAINS ON THE LONDON UNDERGROUND

MALCOLM BATTEN

AMBERLEY

First published 2023

Amberley Publishing
The Hill, Stroud
Gloucestershire, GL5 4EP

www.amberley-books.com

The right of Malcolm Batten to be identified as the Author of this work has been asserted in accordance with the Copyrights, Designs and Patents Act 1988.

ISBN 978 1 3981 1529 3 (print)
ISBN 978 1 3981 1530 9 (ebook)

British Library Cataloguing in Publication Data.
A catalogue record for this book is available from the British Library.

Typesetting by SJmagic DESIGN SERVICES, India.
Printed in the UK.

Introduction

Ninety years ago, in 1933, London's buses, trams, trolleybuses and Underground network were placed under a common ownership when the London Passenger Transport Board was formed, trading as London Transport. The world's largest municipal transport organisation, it acquired a heritage of omnibus transport dating back to 1829 when George Shillibeer first brought horse buses to London; and the world's first underground railway system arrived with the original section of the Metropolitan Railway opening in 1863. This was built to main line gauge on a 'cut and cover' system and of course initially used steam locomotives as electric traction had not then been developed. Recognition of this heritage had already begun under one of London Transport's chief antecedents – the London General Omnibus Company. They had retained one of the famous B type buses of the First World War period along with some of its successors and had celebrated the centenary of omnibuses in 1929 by constructing a replica of Shillibeer's horse bus. London Transport continued this tradition by retaining other historic items, including the last remaining Beyer Peacock 4-4-0T locomotive that worked on the Metropolitan Railway before electrification in 1905. This had survived by being used on the remote Brill branch until this closed in 1935 and then in departmental use until 1948. However, while a growing collection of artefacts was being put aside, there was no museum to display them.

This situation changed in 1961 when the first part of the Museum of British Transport opened in the former Clapham bus (originally tram) garage on 29 March 1961. It was divided into six galleries, featuring models, paintings, maps, tickets, uniforms and other miscellanea. One gallery was entitled 'London on wheels'. In the rear yard, some of the pre-war buses saved by London Transport, of K, S and NS types were displayed at the time.

A Centenary Display was held at Neasden Underground Depot in 1963 to mark 100 years of the Underground. On show were a selection of steam and electric locomotives and rolling stock classes. Beyer Peacock class 'A' No. 23 was restored to 1903 condition with open cab for the occasion. No. 23 would afterwards be moved to Clapham when the second part of the Museum of British Transport opened on 29 May 1963. Also emanating from London Transport came an 1872 Aveling & Porter chain drive geared 0-4-0 originally from the Wotton Tramway. This had been stored at Neasden since 1951 after later working at a brickworks in Northamptonshire. This new part of the museum also exhibited various former railway locomotives, plus trams and buses, many coming from the London Transport collection.

In the earlier days of the 1950s and 1960s, as British Railways started to withdraw steam classes and close lines, there had been ever-increasing numbers of rail tours organised by groups such as the Stephenson Locomotive Society and Locomotive Club of Great Britain. Sometimes these featured the surface Underground lines and LT steam or electric locomotives. For instance, the 'John Milton Special' on 3 June 1956 ran 'top and tailed' by electric locomotives No. 2 *Thomas Lord* and No. 14 *Benjamin Disraeli* from New Cross Gate to Baker Street. The special later continued to Chesham, being hauled from Rickmansworth by LT 0-4-4T No. L48. Metropolitan line compartment stock was used.

On 7 April 1962 the LCGB 'Great Eastern Suburban Rail Tour' from Liverpool Street visited several former GER branches including that to Ongar. This had become part of the Underground Central line under the New Works Programme, but the single-track section from Epping to Ongar had only been electrified in 1957. For this section the train was hauled by ex-GER J15 class 0-6-0 No. 65476. This class continued to work freight over the line until 1962 when diesels took over until freight was withdrawn in the mid-1960s.

In 1971 London Transport finally withdrew their last steam locomotives, three years after British Railways had dispensed with main line steam. Thirteen former GWR 0-6-0PTs had been acquired between 1956 and 1963 to replace the older Metropolitan and District Railway engines. These were used on maintenance trains and trip workings of spoil from Neasden to Croxley Tip near Watford. Withdrawal came because, with the end of BR steam, they could no longer receive heavy overhauls at BR workshops. The last steam-hauled maintenance train ran on 4 June. Requests for a steam-hauled passenger train to mark the end were turned down, but on 6 June No. L94 (formerly GWR/BR No. 7752) worked a demonstration maintenance train from Barbican to Neasden. This last run was a well-publicised event and thousands turned out to witness this. The locomotive was not retained by London Transport, but six of the 0-6-0PTs including L94 passed into private preservation. L94 itself was bought by 7029 Clun Castle Ltd, the owning group behind the Birmingham Railway Museum at Tyseley Locomotive Works.

The Museum of British Transport closed in 1973 as the BR rail exhibits were removed to the new National Railway Museum at York. A replacement museum known as the London Transport Collection opened at Syon Park in 1973. Railway exhibits comprised the Metropolitan 4-4-0T No. 23, the Aveling & Porter geared loco, Metropolitan electric loco No. 5 *John Hampden* and a Q23 type motor car from the District line, along with a selection of buses, etc.

This was replaced by the London Transport Museum at Covent Garden, which opened in 1980. The preserved buses could also sometimes be seen at events such as the HCVC London to Brighton Historic Commercial Vehicle Run, first held in 1962. Other bus rallies began to be organised in the 1970s as private preservation of buses developed. In 1979, the 150 years of London Buses was marked with a rally in Battersea Park and other events. However, other than the stock exhibited at Covent Garden, the other Underground stock retained for preservation could only be seen at the occasional depot open day.

When British Rail dispensed with main line steam in 1968, they had imposed a steam ban on their tracks. This was lifted from 1971, with steam excursions then permitted over certain lighter-used routes. This did not include the London area except on a few special occasions until regular steam excursions started from Marylebone in 1985 and remained banned over the third rail electrified lines of the Southern Region until the early 1990s. When steam ended on the Underground few could have imagined it returning for enthusiast 'specials' over such an intensive network and one with electrified tracks. But they would be wrong!

The first breakthrough into loco-hauled heritage operations came in 1982. The Underground had operated a batch of electric locomotives on the Metropolitan line that hauled trains to Rickmansworth until 1961 when electrification was extended to Amersham and Chesham. One of these locomotives, No. 5 *John Hampden*, had been preserved, being displayed initially at Syon Park and then at Covent Garden. However, another of the class, No. 12 *Sarah Siddons*, had been retained as a brake block test locomotive. Despite earlier denials to the contrary, this was restored in 1981 and worked some tours over its old routes. Over the next few years, it also attended a number of British Rail open days and was adapted to run tours over the Southern Region third rail network.

But the big breakthrough came in 1989. To celebrate the 100 years of the Chesham branch London Underground Ltd (LUL), the successor to London Transport announced that steam trains would run between Chesham and Watford on two successive weekends. This was considered a great success and steam returned next year. In fact, 'Steam on the Met' became a regular annual event, held most years until 2000, evolving with new features and a wealth of different visiting locomotives. What seemed remarkable was that these operations were taking place at weekends amid the normal train operations, which also included Chiltern Line trains over the section from Harrow-on-the-Hill to Amersham. Furthermore, being later held in May, there was often a cup final or similar match on at Wembley bringing additional passengers to the normal Metropolitan line trains. The visiting locomotives came from a variety of heritage lines and had not all been certified to run over British Rail metals. There were also some steam operations over parts of the District line (also built to main line gauge) and a number of depot open days during these years.

But all good things come to an end, and 2000 brought an end to 'Steam on the Met' and, perhaps, all steam running on the Underground. There were some lean years, but there would be more celebrations to come. There was an open day to celebrate fifty years of Upminster Depot in 2009. *Sarah Siddons* made a return in 2011. The interest in historic tube stock was also recognised with trips on the restored 1938 tube stock and Cravens stock trains.

The major new breakthrough though was 2013, for this would be 150 years of the Underground, and it would be celebrated in style! This led to steam running over the original cut-and-cover tunnel section of the Metropolitan Railway through to Moorgate.

The following year 150 years of what is now the Hammersmith & City line was celebrated. Steam would also return to Chesham, this time to celebrate 125 years since opening.

In the following years there was some intermittent Steam on the Met workings, such as Watford 90 in 2015, but not every year. But with new signalling systems being introduced, the opportunities for such operations were diminishing. In 2019 the District line reached 150 years and an opportunity was taken for a final steam heritage working over a part of this line before the impending new signalling was commissioned.

However, although steam traction is unlikely to feature again, at least on some of the lines over which it has run in the past, this has not meant an end of all heritage train operations. For instance, on Saturday–Sunday 3–4 September 2022 the preserved 1938 tube stock ran special trips for the first time since 2019. This was on the Metropolitan line between Harrow-on-the Hill and Amersham and from Amersham to Watford. The Sunday workings were in connection with the Amersham Old Town annual Heritage Day celebrations, which also included vintage bus rides.

2023 marks 160 years of the Underground. Although no heritage train operations had been announced at the time of writing, various celebrations are taking place and such trains may have occurred by the time of publication.

Also included within this book are two heritage locations that were once part of the London Transport network, namely the Buckinghamshire Railway Centre at Quainton Road, near Aylesbury, and the Epping Ongar Railway. Both have retained links to their past history. There are also former London Transport locomotives and stock preserved elsewhere but these are considered as outside the scope of this book.

Please note that all photographs in this book were taken from legitimate publicly accessible viewpoints. However, some of the footbridges and road bridges that were visited in earlier years were later meshed in or had parapets raised to prevent vandalism and so became unusable for photography. Photographs are by the author except where credited.

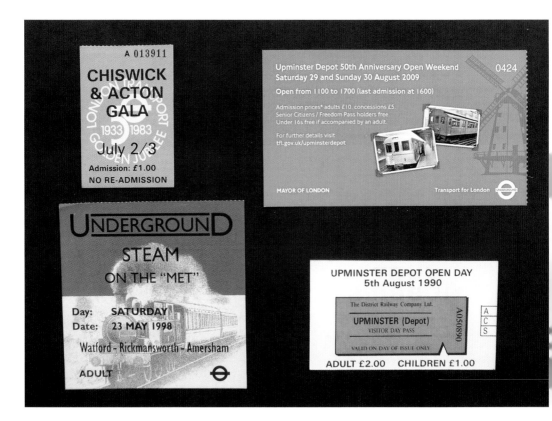

Early Days

Young and old alike enjoy the display of steam and electric stock on display within the confined space of Neasden depot at the Centenary Display held to mark 100 years of the Underground on 25–26 May 1963. The electric locomotive is No. 1 *John Lyon*, named after the founder of Harrow School. There had earlier been a parade of stock for about 1,000 invited guests on 23 May. On 26 May electric locomotive No. 5 *John Hampden* worked an enthusiast's special from Baker Street to Amersham (prior to electrification these had only worked as far as Rickmansworth), where a BR Jubilee class took over to Aylesbury and back. (Geoff Silcock)

One of the steam locomotives on display and still in use at this time for shunting at Neasden and working maintenance trains was 0-6-2T No. L52. After withdrawal in 1962 there was an initial intention to purchase this for preservation, but it was found to have a cracked mainframe and in the end 0-4-4T No. L44 was chosen instead. No. L44 was also at the Neasden Centenary parade hauling four Chesham branch coaches and restored milk van No. 3. (Geoff Silcock)

The preserved Metropolitan Railway 1886 Beyer Peacock 4-4-0T No. 23 was also on display at Neasden, but afterwards was transferred to become an exhibit at the Museum of British Transport at Clapham. When withdrawn in 1948 as No. L45 it was London Transport's oldest locomotive. (Reg Batten)

Also on display at Clapham was the former Wotton Tramway Aveling & Porter geared locomotive. This line, from Quinton Road to Brill, was built privately in 1870–72 for agricultural and industrial use by the third Duke of Buckingham and Chandos, who lived at Wotton House. The line also opened as a public railway. In 1899 the Metropolitan Railway acquired a lease on the line by now run by the Oxford & Aylesbury Tramway Company, who had obtained powers to extend the line to Oxford but failed to raise the money for this. The extension never happened, and the line was closed by London Transport on 30 November 1935. (Reg Batten)

1971: The End of Steam

The end of London Transport steam. The final demonstration freight train headed by 0-6-0PT No. L94 approaches Farringdon on 6 June 1971. It is running on the 'Widened Lines' used by BR suburban trains to Moorgate at the time while the Underground running tracks are to the left. It travelled to Neasden, where there was a rolling stock exhibition held at the depot. (Geoff Silcock)

London Transport Collection, Syon Park

After the Museum of British Transport closed, No. 23 was moved to the new London Transport Collection at Syon Park, where it is seen ahead of a District line Q23 stock coach in May 1977.

Also displayed at Syon Park for the first time was electric locomotive No. 5 *John Hampden*.

London Transport Museum, Covent Garden

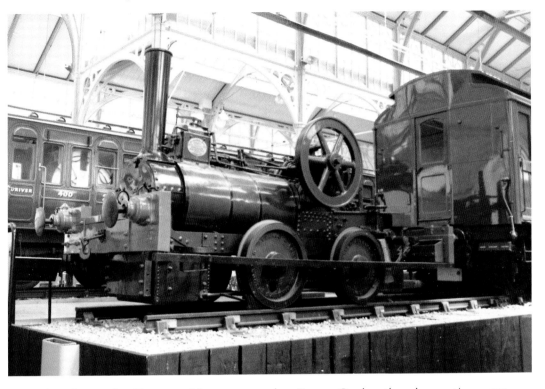

When the London Transport Museum opened at Covent Garden, these locomotives were transferred there, along with the Aveling & Porter geared locomotive. May 1980.

Sarah Siddons Returns

Sarah Siddons enters Croxley on a special train, having come from Watford, and is headed for Amersham on 5 September 1982. This was its first railtour on the Underground after restoration in 1981.

Sarah Siddons on the special returning to Wembley Park pauses at Rickmansworth. The coaching stock was British Rail Mark 2 carriages.

Sarah Siddons was modified to also work over the Southern Region third rail tracks. On 21 September 1985 it hauled an excursion from Victoria to Folkestone West for passengers to visit the Romney, Hythe & Dymchurch Railway. The LT style destination board reads 'New Romney via Folkestone West'. Here it awaits departure from Victoria.

The train is seen a little later passing Beckenham Junction.

A rail show was held at Windsor & Eton Riverside station on 10 December 1989 to celebrate 125 years of the line. As part of the events *Sarah Siddons* worked the 'Magna Carta' trips between Windsor and Staines. Here No. 12 comes off the Windsor line and enters Staines station.

Later in the day the LT locomotive is seen awaiting departure from the Windsor terminus.

Sarah Siddons attended a number of British Rail Open Days and is seen on this occasion 'under the wires' at the Ilford Depot Open Day held on 20 May 1989. The white board on the front reads 'Director of Mechanical Engineering. Brake Block Test Locomotive'.

Also displayed at Ilford was battery locomotive No. 18, brake van No. B583 and a former District line R stock motor coach No. 22679. The R stock consisted of several batches built or converted between 1938 and 1959. Although externally fairly similar to the earlier CO/CP stock the R stock had all cars powered. Those built from 1949 had aluminium, rather than steel, bodies. They lasted until 1983. Beyond this is a Q stock coach.

1983 Acton Works/Chiswick Open Day

An open day was held at Acton Works, along with the adjoining Chiswick bus works, on 2–3 July 1983, as part of the celebrations to mark fifty years of London Transport. *Sarah Siddons* was of course on display, next to Sentinel 0-6-0 diesel locomotive No. DL81, built in 1968 and since itself withdrawn and sold into preservation. Three of these locomotives, DL81–3, were bought second-hand by LT in 1971 to replace the last of the 0-6-0PTs.

Various items were on display that were then still in service but would subsequently be preserved as part of the London Transport Museum collection. Among these was electric sleet locomotive ESL No. 107. This had been converted in 1939 from 1903 ex-Central London Railway motor cars. Working in pairs, the intermediate trailing bogies carried de-icing brushes, ice crushers and spraying gear while the bodies house two 340-litre tanks of antifreeze. Yellow replaced the original maroon livery as an aid to staff safety.

Also present was electric sleet locomotive ESL No. 118A, which had been converted in 1961 from former T stock car 2758.

Shown under restoration was the former District line Q35 stock trailer car 08063.

1989 Chesham Branch Centenary, Saturday/Sunday 1–2 and 8–9 July

The start of 'Steam on the Met' was in 1989 to celebrate the centenary of the Chesham branch. Highlight of the event was Metropolitan Railway 0-4-4T No. 1 (LT No. L44), built in 1898 at Neasden. This had been bought for preservation at the instigation of then nineteen-year-old LT mechanical engineering apprentice Jim Stringer when he found that LT were not planning to retain any of their older steam locomotives themselves. A replacement for the original choice of 0-6-2T No. L52, this was bought for £450. After storage at various sites, it was given a permanent home at Quainton Road in 1970 by the Quainton Railway Society Ltd (now the Buckinghamshire Railway Centre).

The other steam standby locomotive was intended to be the former 0-6-0PT No. L99, now back in GWR livery as No. 7715 and also based at Quainton Road. Both locomotives were examined to British Rail specifications but while No. 1 passed satisfactorily, the boiler inspector ordered all of No. 7715's firebox stays to be replaced together with about 100 rivets. This could not be completed in time and so another Quainton Road-based locomotive, 94XX 0-6-0PT No. 9466, which was passed for main line operation, was substituted.

As LUL had no experience with steam passenger operations, and the option of hiring steam crews from the main line was considered too expensive, it was agreed with HM Railway Inspectorate that the steam loco owners could drive their engines provided they were accompanied by a LUL driver and qualified Operations Inspector. Crew training and a night test run took place in June. The trains ran between Watford and Chesham, with a morning train from Wembley Park and evening return trip.

Met No. 1 approaches Croxley on 9 July. Coaching stock comprised a BR Southern Region 4-VEP EMU in Network SouthEast livery and a support coach.

At the same location is 0-6-0PT No. 9466 on 1 July. Although this was only intended to be a stand-by locomotive with just the occasional run as a condition of it's being made available, in fact No. 1 had run a hot axlebox on the test train and so No. 9466 handled the whole of the first weekend's trains while Met No. 1's axlebox was repaired at the Ffestiniog Railway's workshops. This work was completed in time for No. 1 to work the second weekend.

No. 9466 enters Chalfont & Latimer on 1 July.

The trains ran 'top & tailed' as there are no run-round facilities at either terminus. No. 9466 is on the rear near Northwood on 1 July returning to Wembley Park.

Sarah Siddons was on the other end of the trains, here leading and passing through Croxley towards Watford on 1 July.

Sarah Siddons is on the rear as a train for Chesham passes through Chalfont & Latimer. (Reg Batten)

1990 Steam Harrow-on-the Hill, Amersham

The success of 1989 prompted another steam event in on two weekends in July 1990. This time trains ran between Harrow and Amersham. Met No. 1 and No. 9466 returned and this time they were joined by BR 4MT 2-6-4T No. 80080. *Sarah Siddons* was replaced by battery locomotive No. L44.

No. 9466, Met No. 1, battery loco No. L44 triple-head a train at Chorleywood on 22 July.

BR 4MT 2-6-4T No. 80080 running bunker first at Rickmansworth on 29 July.

Left: No. 80080 heads north near Northwood on 29 July.

Below: Coaching stock this time was a class 305 EMU from the Liverpool Street suburban lines in Network SouthEast livery plus two ex-BR coaches. Displaying 'B. Stortford' on the blinds, No. 305513 is on the rear as a train heads south from Chorleywood on 22 July.

1990 Open Days

The autumn of 1990 would see three depot open days, at Upminster, Ruislip and Morden, the first of these including the opportunity to see steam operation over a different part of the surface stock lines. Ruislip Depot has a direct connection to the British Rail Chiltern Line, which is the usual access point for deliveries of new or refurbished stock. When an open day was held here in October this enabled a selection of main line heritage locomotives to also be displayed and operated at the depot.

An open day at the District line's Upminster Depot on 5 August 1990 saw steam trips between Barking and Upminster. This section of the District line had been transferred from the LMS to the Underground in 1932, having originally been constructed by the London, Tilbury & Southend Railway. Met No. 1 passes Hornchurch, one of the additional stations opened by the Underground on the way from Barking to Upminster.

Met No. 1 again en route between Barking and Upminster. (Reg Batten)

Met No. 1 and battery loco No. L44 work shuttles at the Upminster Depot Open Day.

A train of former CO/CP stock on display with car 4416 leading.

In 1986 three two-car units were constructed to test new technology before ordering new stock for the Jubilee Line Extension. Set A was built by Metro-Cammell with GEC equipment and painted red/silver, Set B was built by British Rail Engineering at Derby with Brush equipment and was blue/silver, and Set C was by Metro-Cammell with Brown Boveri equipment and was green/silver. Set B, which became the prototype for the 1992 Central line stock, was displayed at Upminster.

At Ruislip Depot on 28 October ex-City & South London Railway coach 135, dating from 1902 and owned by the London Underground Railway Society, is awaiting restoration.

In the mid-1960s, forty-three vehicles of Standard tube stock, built between 1923 and 1934, were transferred to the Isle of Wight to replace BR steam trains between Ryde and Shanklin. These were replaced by 1938 stock in 1989–90. A five-car train of the Standard stock was formed in 1990 and returned to the Underground ownership. A driving motor car from 4-VEC set 485044 in final Network SouthEast livery was on display at Ruislip, and later also at the Morden Depot Open Day.

Electric sleet locomotive ESL No. 107, which was earlier seen in yellow livery at Acton while still in service, had now been put aside for preservation and was on display at Ruislip.

A two-coach shuttle service through the site was unusually top-and-tailed by Met No. 1 and preserved BR Deltic No. D9000 *Royal Scots Grey*. Another Class 55 Deltic was also on static display – No. D9016 *Gordon Highlander*.

Two cars of the Standard tube stock brought back from the Isle of Wight were repainted into Underground colours before shipping. Former IOW car 27 is in 1920s livery with maroon doors as seen at Morden Depot on 4 November.

Trailer car 44
carries 1930s
livery with red
doors. Note
the car still in
Network SE livery
next to it.

A four-car set
of 1938 stock
provided a shuttle
service between
Morden station
and the depot.

Seen from the
road bridge
opposite the
station, the 1938
stock heads away
to the depot.

1990 Central Line Cravens Stock

Despite the rundown of the Epping–Ongar section of the Central line, the 125th anniversary of the opening of the line was celebrated in 1990. A spotless train of Cravens stock in red livery was used and a good turnout by locals and enthusiasts is evident in this view at North Weald. The passing loop had been redundant since the introduction of a one-train service in 1976 and was lifted in July 1978. By 1990 only three three-car sets remained of the 1960-built Cravens stock (now with 1938 stock trailers) and two of these were repainted red for the Epping–Ongar shuttle in 1990–91. (Alan Simpson)

1991 Northern Line Stock

In 1990, to celebrate 100 years of electric tube railways of which part of the original City & South London Railway is included in the Northern line, a train of the line's 1959 stock was repainted into 1923 style livery and given 1920s style moquette upholstery. It re-entered service on 19 July.

The repainted stock enters Burnt Oak station on 6 March 1991.

The stock is seen again against the 1930s architecture of East Finchley station on 15 December 1991.

1992 Steam Harrow-on-the Hill, Amersham

There was no steam event in 1991, but it returned for 1992, which marked the centenary of railways to Amersham. No.1 was unavailable so two new locomotives were invited, LMS 'Black Five' 4-6-0 No. 44932 and LNER N7 0-6-2T No. 69621. Stock now comprised coaches from ex-BR 4TC push-pull unit 8015 and 4-REP 1901, which LUL had acquired and painted in maroon. The dates changed from July to the last two weekends of May, including bank holiday Monday.

Above: The N7 and *Sarah Siddons* approach Chorleywood on 25 May. (Reg Batten)

Right: The N7 steams through the countryside as it approaches Chorleywood on 25 May. Note the GER style headboard reading Verney Junction, north of Aylesbury – and once the furthest point reached by the former Metropolitan Railway.

The N7 passes through Chorleywood with a staff excursion, hence the lack of enthusiasts evident on the platforms. The headboard reads 'Amersham Centenary 1892–1992'. (Geoff Silcock)

The N7 crosses the Grand Union Canal near Watford as a narrow boat waits to enter the lock. (Geoff Silcock)

'Black Five' No. 44932 passes Chalfont & Latimer. (Reg Batten)

1993 Ruislip Depot Open Day

Preserved Class 20 No. D8110 is nicely posed outside the depot on 16 May 1993.

Also nicely posed was visiting BR 7MT 4-6-2 No. 70000 *Britannia*.

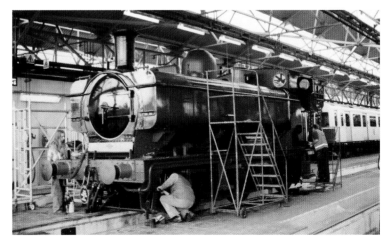

Inside the depot, one of the GWR Pannier tanks was being repainted ready for Steam on the Met duties.

1993 Steam on the Met: Saturday–Sunday 22–23 May and Saturday–Monday 29–31 May

Steam was back for 1993 and now the programme introduced the 'Steam on the Met' branding. This year saw two of the former LT pannier tanks, both in LT livery – No. L90 (No. 7760) and No. L99 (No. 7715). They were joined by LMS 2MT 2-6-0 No. 46441. *Sarah Siddons* was also back and joined by Class 20 diesel No. 20227, on hire to London Underground for the Metropolitan line Track Replacement Project. These locomotives provided air brake facilities. A four-coach train service ran from Watford to Amersham stopping at Rickmansworth on the first weekend. Here, vintage buses connected with Rickmansworth Canal 200 events. On the second weekend trains ran from Harrow-on-the-Hill to Amersham and back non-stop with a seven-coach formation. Steam locomotives were changed on each trip at Amersham on both weekends where run-round facilities were available.

L99, formerly GWR and BR No. 7715, approaches Croxley on 22 May.

The two panniers are seen double-heading, passing Northwood Hills on 30 May.

Returning from Amersham, the two panniers plus *Sarah Siddons* approach Moor Park on 31 May.

Ivatt 2MT 2-6-0 No. 46441 was painted in this fictitious BR maroon livery, slightly lighter than the LT red of the panniers. Here it passes Moor Park on 30 May.

Running tender first, No. 46441 and Class 20 No. 20227 pass through Croxley on 22 May.

One of the pannier tanks is seen crossing the Grand Union Canal. (Reg Batten)

Class 20 No. 20227 at Amersham on 22 May. Note the headboard!

1993 Steam Ealing Broadway, West Kensington

The following weekend No. L99 and *Sarah Siddons* ventured on new grounds to run seven trips each day between Ealing Broadway and West Kensington to mark 125 years of the District Railway.

No. L99 brings the stock into Ealing Common station on 5 June.

Ealing Broadway is served by both the District line and Central line. Here No. L99 stands at one of the District line platforms as a train of 1959 tube stock forms a Central line train. (Reg Batten)

No. L99 makes a fine sight in a cutting near Ealing Common on 5 June.

Sarah Siddons amid some more classic London Underground architecture as it passes through Ealing Common station on 5 June.

Sarah Siddons again, near Ealing Common, on 5 June.

Sarah Siddons threads the complex junction on the west side of Acton Town station on 5 June.

Sarah Siddons again, and this time the location is West Kensington, again on 5 June.

1994 Steam on the Met: Saturday–Sunday 21–22 May and Saturday–Monday 28–30 May

1994 marked the ninetieth anniversary of the line from Harrow to Uxbridge and trains ran to Uxbridge, as well as between Harrow and Amersham. Steam locomotives featured were No. L99, BR 4MT 2-6-4T No. 80079 and LNER N2 0-6-2T No. 69523. A school party trip also ran on Friday 20 May and a staff family trip on Friday 27 May. As there are facilities for locomotives to run round at Harrow and Amersham this allowed for locomotives to be changed at Amersham on each trip. There was an open day at Rickmansworth Depot on the first weekend, while on the first Sunday BR Class 121 single-unit DMU 55013 was hired to work on the Chesham branch as the 'Chesham Bubble'.

One train ran in the morning each day 28–30 May from Harrow to Uxbridge and back. *Sarah Siddons* passes through Ruislip Manor on the Uxbridge branch, with the return trip on 30 May. The headboard reads 'Harrow–Uxbridge 1904–1994'.

No. L99 produces a fine smoke display as it speeds through Chorleywood with its restored signal box on 30 May.

Bound for Harrow-on-the-Hill, in the opposite direction comes N2 No. 69523 at Chorleywood on 30 May.

BR 4MT 2-6-4T No. 80079 passes Moor Park northbound on 30 May.

No. L99 again, making easy work of its train in full sunshine. (Geoff Silcock)

1995 Steam on the Met

A new innovation for 1995 was parallel running of the first trains to Watford and Amersham on the four-track section north of Harrow-on-the-Hill. Trains ran from Harrow to Watford or Amersham, and there was a morning train to Uxbridge and back. Locomotives featured were No. 9466 and No. 80079 on return visits and a new entry, BR 4MT 4-6-0 No. 75014. *Sarah Siddons* suffered a hot axlebox and was replaced by battery loco No. L17, while No. 20227 was also in use again. With the increasing popularity of these events LUL had purchased three additional coaches – Mark IIB stock from BR.

BR Class 4 4-6-0 No. 75014 plus *Sarah Siddons* bring the empty stock up from Neasden Depot to Harrow-on-the-Hill at the start of the day's operations and pass through Preston Road on 21 May. The headboard reads 'Watford branch 1925–1995'.

The following week No. 80079 brings the empty stock through Northwick Park on 28 May.

A freshly painted battery loco No. L17 is on the back of the other train of empty stock hauled by No. 75014 as it passes Northwick Park on 28 May.

Class 20 No. 20227 takes the fast non-platform line at Northwick Park returning the stock on 28 May.

Left: A major feature of the 1995 event was the parallel running of the first trains to Watford and Amersham on the four-track section north of Harrow-on-the-Hill. No. 75014 and No. 80079 make a dramatic scene as they storm north. (Geoff Silcock)

Below: No. 9466 plus L17 at Moor Park on 28 May.

No. 75014 heads north past Moor Park on 29 May.

No. 9466 and No. L17 depart from Amersham on 29 May.

No. 80079 plus No. 20227 seen departing Amersham on 29 May.

1995 *Sarah Siddons* to Stanmore

Sarah Siddons was able to work with the 4TC coaches in push-pull mode and ran some separate tours in this way, such as the 'Metro Rover' in February 1995 and 'Metro Ranger' in March 1996. Here it is on the rear of 'The Stanmore Klondyker' at Queensbury on 10 September 1995.

Working in push-pull mode, this is the driving end of the 4TC stock. The Stanmore branch had originally been built as part of the Metropolitan line and thus could take main line profile stock.

1996 Steam on the Met

In 1996 the service was revised as Watford–Amersham with the first and last trains starting and finishing at Harrow. Again, parallel running featured. Steam locomotives were No. 9466, No. 75014 and new entry GWR 2-6-0 No. 7325. *Sarah Siddons* and No. 20227 were also in use again. The Rickmansworth Depot Open Day moved to the second weekend to avoid clashing with the canal festival.

GWR 2-6-0 No. 7325 plus No. 20227 bring the empty stock from Neasden through Northwick Park on 18 May.

The other set of stock is headed through Northwick Park by No. 75014, back for a second year, again on 18 May.

Parallel running took place again and here No. 7325 and No. 9466 head the respective trains for Watford and Amersham through Moor Park on 27 May.

1996 Heritage Stock to Stanmore

The Cravens stock train, which had worked the last service on the Epping–Ongar branch when it closed in September 1994, was bought for preservation by Cravens Heritage Trains and operated some enthusiast specials over the LUL network. Here it passes Kingsbury on 18 August 1996.

The Cravens stock seen again at Canons Park on 18 August.

This was in connection with an open day at Stanmore where the repainted Northern line stock and *Sarah Siddons* were among the exhibits on display.

1998 Steam on the Met: Saturday–Sunday 16–17 May and Saturday–Monday 23–25 May

There was no Steam on the Met in 1997, but it returned for 1998. Four steam locomotives featured: No. 9466, GWR 41XX 2-6-2T No. 4144 from Didcot, LMS 2-6-0 No. 2968 from the Severn Valley Railway and LNER B1 4-6-0 No. 1264 *Mayflower* from the Great Central Railway. No. 9466 was brought in as a replacement for *Mayflower* when it suffered a boiler defect, although this was later rectified for the second weekend. Once again *Sarah Siddons* and No. 20227 provided air braking. A variation this year was parallel running between the first steam train from Harrow and a scheduled Metropolitan line train as far as Moor Park. Trains then ran between Watford and Amersham stopping at Rickmansworth. Buses from here linked to the Canal Festival on 16–17 May. There was also an open day at Rickmansworth depot with preserved trains, buses, etc. on 23–25 May. Coach trips ran from Amersham to attractions including the Chiltern Open Air Museum and John Milton's Cottage.

GWR 2-6-2T No. 4144 and the support coach pass Northwick Park on 25 May.

No. 4144 plus No. 20227 pause at Rickmansworth on 24 May.

The sole surviving Stainer 2-6-0 No. 2968 brings its train through the platforms at Croxley and will then turn north for Amersham on 24 May.

No. 2968 departs from Amersham on 25 May as B1 No. 1264 and No. 9466 wait to take over the following train.

B1 No. 1264 plus No. 9466 pass Chorleywood on 25 May.

The B1 approaches Croxley from Watford on 23 May.

1999 Steam on the Met: Saturday–Sunday 22–23 May and Saturday–Monday 29–31 May

For 1999 again four steam locomotives featured, three of them for the first time. Along with No. 9466 there was the first Southern Railway locomotive, U class 2-6-0 No. 31625 from the Mid Hants Railway, LMS 'Black Five' No. 45110 and LNER K1 2-6-0 No. 62005, thus one from each of the 'Big Four' companies that formed British Railways. Met No. 1, needing an overhaul, was on display at Rickmansworth to mark its centenary. After the initial parallel running steam trains from Harrow, the service ran between Watford and Amersham, calling at Rickmansworth. Buses from here linked to the Canal Festival on 22–23 May. There was also a display of traction engines at Rickmansworth and Amersham stations and an open day at Rickmansworth depot with preserved trains, buses, etc. on 29–31 May. Coach trips ran from Amersham to attractions including the Chiltern Open Air Museum and John Milton's Cottage.

No. 9466 plus No. 20227 are in action again at Croxley on 23 May. The headboard this time read 'Steam on the Met 1989–1999' to mark ten years of these activities.

A newcomer for 1999 was Southern U class 2-6-0 No. 31625, seen at the familiar location of Croxley on 23 May.

Above: U class No. 31265, seen again near Chorleywood on 30 May.

Right: No. 31625 is caught crossing the Grand Union Canal bridge. (Geoff Silcock)

Also making a debut appearance, 'Black Five' No. 45110 plus No. 9466 are departing Rickmansworth northbound on 30 May.

The location at Croxley had gradually become more cluttered over the years and now these overrun marker posts had been installed, one of which can be seen on the left as the locomotive approaches on 23 May.

A welcome visitor for 1999, not normally seen in the south of Britain, was the sole surviving Peppercorn K1 2-6-0 No. 62005, again at Croxley on 29 May.

The K1 makes a fine sight departing north from Rickmansworth on 30 May.

1999–2000 Heritage Tube Stock in Action

The repainted Northern line stock stops at Finchley Central on 2 April 1999. Contrast the Great Northern Railway architecture of this station on the High Barnet branch, incorporated into the Underground under the 1935 New Works Programme, with that of the previous station, East Finchley (see p. 30).

The Cravens stock visited Chesham on 21 May 2000. Note the water tower and signal box, survivors from the steam age. The alignment of the former run-round loop is also clear. When the line was built by the Great Central Railway it was originally intended to continue on to a junction with the London & North Western Railway, but this never happened.

Another view at Chesham on 21 May 2000. Note the signal box, no longer needed, but nicely restored.

2000 Steam on the Met

2000 was the last year of the annual Steam on the Met operations. Stalwart No. 9466 was back again, as was KI No. 62005 for a second year. New appearances were by LMS Ivatt 2MT 2-6-2T No. 41312 from the Mid Hants Railway and LNER B12 No. 61572 from the North Norfolk Railway.

However, this was to be the last of the annual Steam on the Met events. The division of London Underground into separate infrastructure and operating companies, and a feeling that these events were diverting resources away from the core business, led to a decision to bring this to an end. It seems almost surreal, looking back in hindsight, that such an operation, over busy lines, shared in part with Chiltern Line trains, and held on weekends when there was often a major sporting event at Wembley, would even have been sanctioned as any breakdown could have had huge knock-on effects. Unlike on heritage railways, these steam trains had to be driven at speeds of up to 50 mph to keep to the timings in between the service trains. But with dedication and professionalism it all worked superbly.

No. 9466 back yet again, but paired with a newcomer, Ivatt 2MT 2-6-2T No. 41312, at Croxley on 29 May.

The pair, plus No. 20227, form a triple-header travelling south from Chorleywood on 21 May.

Making its debut was the only surviving inside-cylinder 4-6-0, the GER design B12 No. 61572 from the North Norfolk Railway. Again, the location is Croxley on 27 May.

The B12 heads north at Rickmansworth on 21 May. The other train has just passed heading south (luckily not getting in the way of the photograph!). A pair of battery locos are parked up in one of the sidings to complete the scene.

Right: K1 No. 62005 drifts into Amersham on 21 May.

Below: No. 20227 was on hand again, but now painted in a maroon Metropolitan-style livery. This is displayed as it stands on arrival at Watford on 27 May.

2000s London Transport Museum Depot and London Transport Museum

The London Transport Museum has been housed at Covent Garden since 1980, ideally sited in the heart of London to catch the all-important tourist trade. It has had two rebuilds since then, including the creation of a mezzanine floor.

The London Transport Museum Depot at Acton opened in October 1999. This houses the reserve collection not on display at Covent Garden and is the base for curation and conservation. It is connected to the Underground so that railway stock such as the heritage 1938 tube stock can access the network. Unlike Covent Garden it is not open to the public daily but only on certain weekends each year.

The City & South London Railway was the first deep-level tube line and the first to use electricity when it opened in 1890. Locomotive haulage was used at first and one of the original diminutive locomotives has survived and is now on display at Acton. No. 13 was built by Mather & Platt, Salford Iron Works, Manchester, in 1890. 5 March 2006.

Sarah Siddons at the London Transport Museum Depot on 8 March 2008, now repainted in earlier Metropolitan livery. In 2012 this would visit the National Railway Museum at York, along with former 0-6-0PT No. L94.

Electric sleet locomotive ESL No. 107, which we saw earlier (see p. 26) is now restored and on display at Acton.

Also displayed at Acton is one car from the 1986 experimental Set C (see p. 25).

No. 140242. The first section of the Victoria line opened in 1968. The original 1967 stock has been replaced but one of the trains has been retained at Acton.

The interior of a Q23 stock car, preserved in the London Transport Museum at Covent Garden.

2011 Heritage Stock in Action

Following its repaint *Sarah Siddons* was back in action on 22 May 2011. It was photographed at Croxley travelling towards Amersham. A Class 20 was on the other end of the train.

Sarah Siddons crosses the Grand Union Canal near Watford as a narrow boat enters the canal basin. Note the carriages have now been repainted in a mock teak effect style.

Working with *Sarah Siddons* were a pair of Class 20s. No. 20189 is the leading locomotive as a train for Watford passes through Croxley.

A four-car set of 1938 tube stock was retained as a heritage unit and has seen occasional use on tours. This was also running on this day and is also seen at Croxley on 22 May.

The 1938 stock loads in the platform at Watford. Because the station is normally served by the Metropolitan line stock built to main line gauge, there is a step down from the platform to the train.

The 1938 stock at Turnham Green on 19 June 2011. Although the front blinds say Piccadilly line, the train is travelling on the District line track, while a Piccadilly line train is on the parallel track. At most times the Piccadilly line trains do not stop at the stations between Hammersmith and Acton Town, which are also served by the District line.

2013 Underground 150: Kensington Olympia–Moorgate Sunday 13 and 20 January

2013 marked 150 years since the first part of the Metropolitan Railway opened between Paddington and Farringdon. Planning for how to celebrate this began in 2010 and soon revolved around reviving steam operations, only this time including the sub-service original tunnel sections. As part of the planning for the 2013 events, on 26 February 2012 the National Railway Museum's L&SWR Beattie 0-4-0WT No. 30587 was borrowed from the Bodmin & Wenford Railway and tested at night to see if steam operation was possible through the Circle line tunnels.

Met No. 1 was an obvious choice for the 2013 events, but the boiler ticket had expired in 2009. An inspection showed that it would be capable of doing the job required with restoration and the contract for this went to Bill Parker's Flour Mill workshop in the Dean Forest, which had undertaken the previous overhaul. After overhaul, the Avon Valley Railway hosted Met No. 1 as it was run in. The Severn Valley Railway then tested the locomotive at up to 50 mph.

One of the highlights was the restoration and use of four-wheel 'Jubilee' Metropolitan Railway coach 353 of 1892. This had survived in final use as a garden shed before being offered to the London Transport Museum in 1974. Restoration took place at the Ffestiniog Railway. As the original chassis had long gone it was mounted on a modified former Southern Railway parcels van chassis. It was then tested at up to 50 mph at the Great Central Railway. As well as being used on the Underground, this also later visited the heritage railways that had either been part of the Underground or had contributed in some way to the celebrations. It also took part in the Lord Mayor's Show (on a low-loader). The Bluebell Railway sent their four wooden-bodied Ashbury coaches that used to work on the Chesham branch before electrification.

Test runs were made at night before the public events took place.

At the start of the day's running on 13 January, *Sarah Siddons* draws the train out of Lillie Bridge depot towards Kensington Olympia. I recall that standing on the road bridge waiting for this; the weather was bitterly cold, about -3 degrees as recorded by a digital thermometer display on a nearby hoarding. On 20 January there was lying snow on the ground.

Met No. 1 brings the first train back from Olympia at 10.54 a.m., carrying 150 invited VIP guests. The stock consisted of restored Metropolitan Railway milk van 3 in the lead. This was followed by car 353. The rest of the train was made up of the four-car Chesham set from the Bluebell Railway. The reason for using this rather than the 4TC set was clearance in some of the tunnel sections. The white lamps carried were borrowed from the A1 Steam Locomotive Trust.

No. 1 on the rear as the train returns to Olympia, photographed from the multistorey car park seen in the background of the previous photo. The headboard reads '150 Underground Pioneer 1863–2013'. The public could ride on this and subsequent trains. Although tickets cost between £150 and £180 for this unique experience, demand was so high that a ballot was held.

2013 Steam on the Met: 25–27 May and 7–8 September

After the success of the January celebrations, steam returned to the previous stamping ground north of Harrow in May. Met No. 1 and another old stalwart 0-6-0PT No. 9466 returned. They were joined by former GWR 2-6-2T No. 5521. Owned by Bill Parker from the Flour Mill, the locomotive was fitted with a Westinghouse air pump and had previously been taken over to Poland in 2007 for their centenary celebrations and where it would work service trains around Wolsztyn. The loco was repainted in London Transport maroon and numbered as L150. Along with *Sarah Siddons*, three privately owned Class 20 diesels were hired, two of which were repainted in Underground-style liveries.

GWR Hawksworth 0-6-0PT No. 9466 made a return visit to Steam on the Met, but now in BR black livery. Here it passes through Chorleywood with *Sarah Siddons*. A new '150' headboard was carried. Taken on 27 May.

Later in the day it is the turn of No. L150 to run through Chorleywood. A bearing on Met No.1 had run hot on its first trip so it was taken out of use for the rest of the weekend.

The stock is brought back south through Chorleywood by Class 20 20189 painted as London Transport L189. Coach 353 is in use but there was no need to bring in the 'Chesham' set on this occasion, so it was paired with a 4TC set.

A second weekend of Steam on the Met took place in September. The stock had started out from Ruislip Depot, which has a connection to the Metropolitan line. Here the stock has just passed through West Harrow on its way to start the day's activities from Harrow-on-the-Hill. At the head is Class 20 No. 20227 in a contemporary Underground livery on 7 September.

Later on 7 September No. L189 approaches Moor Park southbound with No. 20227, No. 9466 and Met No. 1 on the rear.

A rear view as the train passes through the station with Met No. 1 on the rear.

Later in the day, the same combination heads north again through Moor Park.

On the following day Met No. 1 and No. L150 both failed with leaks so No. 9466 performed alone. Here it leads as the stock heads north near Northwood.

The rear view of the same train with No. 20227 on the tail.

A fine display from the chimney as No. 9466 passes Chalfont & Latimer on 8 September.

No. 20227 brings the stock into Rickmansworth on 8 September.

2013 Steam to Uxbridge: Sunday 8 December

On 8 December 2013 steam returned to the Uxbridge branch as six trips were operated between Harrow and Uxbridge. Met No. 1 was the obvious choice as this had worked the first train to Uxbridge when the line opened on 4 July 1904. It worked a test train on 3 December but a leak was spotted from an ancient repair so this was withdrawn. No. L150 came in to replace it, working with *Sarah Siddons* and with a Class 20 on the other end of the train.

A different Class 20 was in use on this occasion as blue-liveried No. 20142 heads through Ruislip Manor station.

A going away view of the train reveals a service train to Uxbridge approaching – lucky it wasn't a few seconds earlier or it would have obscured the photograph!

Later in the day No. L150 and *Sarah Siddons* head for Uxbridge in a sylvan setting near Hillingdon. No. L150 had been modified since its last appearance, with the cab lowered so that it could now also transverse the tunnel sections if required.

No. 20142 again, as it returns the train from Uxbridge near Hillingdon. As with Steam on the Met services to Watford, trains ran top-and-tailed as there are no run-round facilities at Uxbridge.

Locals admire No. L150 as an afternoon Uxbridge-bound train passes under the covered footbridge at Ruislip.

2014 Hammersmith & City 150: Saturday 2 and 9 August

2014 marked 150 years of what is now the Hammersmith & City line, which opened to Hammersmith on 13 June 1864. Initially worked by the Great Western Railway, the Metropolitan ran the trains from 1865. On each day, the first train ran from Northfields, now on the Piccadilly line, to Moorgate. Then three trips from Moorgate to Hammersmith and finally Moorgate back to Northfields. All trains ran non-stop. Met No. 1 hauled the trains eastbound with *Sarah Siddons* hauling the westbound workings. Stock was the same used for the January 2013 services.

At the beginning of the day on 2 August Met No. 1 heads the stock approaching Bayswater on the run up from Northfields. This shows the 'cut-and-cover' construction used in building these early sections of the lines for steam traction.

No. 1 awaits departure from Hammersmith. The milk van is at the head of the train.

A contrast in styles at the buffers of Hammersmith (Met) station.

The service train has departed, and *Sarah Siddons* is fully revealed at the rear of the train in platform 1.

Met No. 1 passes through Westbourne Park. It will then run parallel with the Great Western main line for a short while before tunnelling under to cross to the other side at the next station Royal Oak.

Later in the afternoon, Met No. 1 enters Barbican as it nears journey's end at Moorgate. Note the elevated signal box on the left, since removed.

Sarah Siddons passes through Notting Hill Gate at the end of the day, returning the stock to Northfields. The splendid overall roof dates from the opening of the station in 1868.

On the second weekend, on 9 August, *Sarah Siddons* passes through Farringdon. A Thameslink train on the 'Widened lines' can just be glimpsed to the right.

Plenty of passengers photograph Met No. 1 with their phones as it passes through Ladbroke Grove. Most of them were probably waiting for a normal Hammersmith & City line train rather than being out to photograph the special workings.

It was touch and go but the service train pulled away from Goldhawk Road station just in time to avoid obscuring *Sarah Siddons* on a Hammersmith-bound working.

On a section of the original part of the Metropolitan Railway opened in 1863, Met No. 1 approaches Farringdon on its way to Moorgate on 9 August. (Geoff Silcock)

At the end of the day *Sarah Siddons* appropriately shows a 'Depot' destination as it works the stock back to Northfields and passes through West Kensington.

2014 Chesham 125: Saturday–Sunday 16–17 August

On 16–17 August steam returned to the Chesham branch, where the revival had started in 1989 to celebrate the centenary. This time 125 years was being celebrated. Rather appropriately, the 'Chesham' set of coaches from the Bluebell Railway was hired to once more work over the line where it last worked in service days. The first train each day ran steam hauled from Wembley Park to Rickmansworth. Then trains ran top-and-tailed from Rickmansworth to Chesham, with the last train returning to Harrow. Met No. 1, No. L150 and *Sarah Siddons* provided motive power.

The stock heads north at Northwood on 17 August with No. L150 and *Sarah Siddons* on the front and Met No. 1 on the tail.

At Rickmansworth it was raining heavily so there were few people on the platform to take photos.

The driver of Met No. 1 awaits departure. His high-vis jacket seems somewhat out of place amid the otherwise vintage atmosphere.

2019 District 150: Saturday–Sunday 22–23 June

2015 was meant to feature steam working between Watford and Chesham on 5 and 12 July to celebrate ninety years of Watford station, but this was postponed following the incident with the Cravens stock returning from Epping (see p. 93). However, the trains ran on 12–13 September with services from Harrow to Watford and Chesham again worked by Met No. 1, No. L150 and *Sarah Siddons* with the Chesham set coaches. In 2016 trains were arranged for the District line between Ealing Broadway and High Street Kensington on 9–10 July, the only free weekend between engineering work, but they had to be called off as the Chesham set coaches were under repair at the Bluebell Railway. There were a few other steam workings between 2016 and 2018 but I did not cover these, so we move on to 2019, which marked 150 years of the District line. Three trains each day ran between Ealing Broadway and High Street Kensington with the vintage stock. Met No. 1, at that time working on the Epping Ongar Railway, was provided to work with *Sarah Siddons*.

Metropolitan No. 1 brings the stock through West Kensington at the end of the day, returning the stock to Ealing Common depot on 23 June 2019.

2019 Class 20s to Quainton Road

On bank holiday Monday 26 August 2019 an excursion was operated from Marylebone station to the Buckinghamshire Railway Centre at Quainton Road via Aylesbury. The Underground 4TC stock was used and the stock is seen at Marylebone having been brought in by Class 20s No. 20007 and No. 20142 *Sir John Betjeman*.

A view of No. 20142 in its Metropolitan-style livery. The coaches had also been repainted maroon. Note the LT carriage number on the first coach.

The train was hauled to Quainton Road by preserved Class 33 No. D6515 *Lt Jenny Lewis RN*, seen prior to drawing out the stock and reversing into a platform road. This had also worked an earlier trip to Quainton Road on 29 April and had been fitted with trip cock apparatus, becoming the first of its class to work over LUL metals.

Buckinghamshire Railway Centre, Quainton Road

Two locations that were once part of the London Transport Underground network survive as heritage centres or lines. The Buckinghamshire Railway Centre at Quainton Road, north of Aylesbury, was originally an outpost of the Metropolitan Railway, which extended to its furthest point to Verney Junction. Quainton Road was the junction for the branch to Brill, closed in 1935. The section north of Amersham passed to the LNER in 1937. After the Great Central route north from Aylesbury to Rugby closed in 1966, the station itself closed to passengers in 1963, became the base for the Quainton Railway Society Ltd in 1969. This was joined by the London Railway Preservation Society in 1971 and became the Buckinghamshire Railway Centre on gaining charitable status in 1972.

Quainton Road is the home base for Met No. 1 and here it is on home turf in 2013 as part of the Underground 150 celebrations. Coach 353 is coupled behind it on this occasion on 26 August, along with 1905 Metropolitan Railway 'steam stock' brake third coach 427 and a BR Mark 1 coach.

To mark the 150 years, the Buckinghamshire Railway Centre painted their Andrew Barclay industrial 0-4-0ST *Swanscombe* in Metropolitan livery and renamed it *Brill No.1*. It stands with a pair of vintage carriages, one a replica of the Brill branch coach, at the former Brill branch platform. A proposal to relay about a mile of the line from Quainton Road has been scuppered by the building of HS2, which cuts across the trackbed.

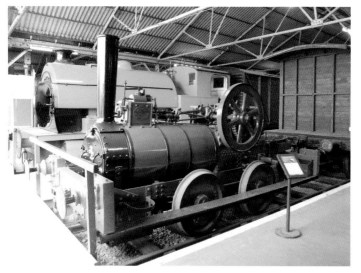

The former Wotton Tramway Aveling & Porter geared loco 'returned home' when it was transferred from the London Transport Museum on loan and is now part of the museum display at Quainton Road.

A former District line three-car CO/CP stock train is displayed at Quainton with car 53028 leading.

Epping Ongar Railway

The former Great Eastern Railway line from Stratford to Ongar via Epping and the Hainault loop were designated to be electrified and become an extension to the Central line under the New Works Programme of 1935. Electrification reached Epping in 1949 when the lined passed to London Transport control. However, the more rural 6-mile extension from Epping to Ongar remained steam worked until electrified in 1957. This lightly used single-track shuttle service was in stark contrast to the busy central London section of the Central line. With mounting losses, closure was first applied for in 1970, but was refused. The line was run down until eventually closure was approved in 1994, on the proviso that the track would be left intact for a heritage group to take it over. After a controversial sale to property developers Pilot Developments, the line would eventually reopen under new management as a steam and diesel heritage line in May 2012. Trains cannot run into Epping station itself as the Central line uses both platforms and it is signalled for automatic train operation.

As a former part of the Underground, the Epping Ongar Railway was fully involved in the 150 years celebrations of 2013. Metropolitan No. 1 visited and is seen here at Marconi Bridge, north of North Weald, with a vintage train including the restored coach 353 and Metropolitan Railway coaches 427 and 509. Prairie tank No. L150 also visited in 2013. Met No. 1 would later return for an extended stay until 2019, and No. L150 returned on long-term loan from 2021.

Left: 2014 marked twenty years since closure of the line, and this was suitably celebrated in September when the last Underground train to work on the line, which had itself been preserved, returned to the railway and once again worked through to Ongar – albeit this time diesel-propelled! The tube cars and diesels were brought in over the surviving connection to the Central line at Epping during the night – the only occasion since reopening that this connection has been used. (Owen Hayward)

Below: The Cravens stock stands in the platform at North Weald with the 'Silent Whistle' headboard as carried in the cab window on the last day. Sharing the duties for the weekend was Met No. 1 making a repeat visit. This also worked a demonstration LT engineering works train through the North Weald station area.

As the EOR is of course no longer electrified the tube train was not taking power but was hauled or propelled by a pair of London Underground's tube profile Schoma diesels. No. 3 *Claire* leads as the stock enters North Weald. Another pair of the Schoma diesels were on display at Ongar. Unfortunately, on the return of the Cravens stock, a shoebeam fractured and fell on the track. This led to a ban being implemented on the movement of heritage stock until an enquiry reported back, which nearly scuppered the 2015 Underground steam schedule.

During 2018 London Underground Ltd donated a 1959 stock driving motor car, No. 1031, as used on the Northern line until 2000. This had been retained at Morden Depot until disposed of due to an upgrade project. The tube car was positioned at North Weald with the intention of it being used for a museum display. However, as a result of asbestos content, no work has been possible on this to date.

The 2021 Steam Gala held on 11–12 September saw a visit by 57XX pannier tank No. 5786 in its London Transport livery as No. L92. This is owned by the Worcester Locomotive Society and normally based on the South Devon Railway. Demonstration freight trains ran to Ongar each day and here No. L92 collects the stock from the siding for the return journey on 11 September.

The climax of the 2021 Gala season was the London Transport Gala held over three days, Friday–Sunday 8–10 October. This featured three locomotives in London Transport livery, probably a first for any heritage railway, along with Class 31 No. 31458. The best of the weather was on the Sunday, and here at North Weald we see Class 20 No. 20227, now renamed *Sherlock Holmes*, in 2018 waiting to depart for Ongar while No. L92 has coupled on to the rear of a train for Epping Forest headed by the Class 31 to haul it back. Note the replica London Transport roundels mounted at the stations for the occasion.

The other LT-liveried locomotive was No. 5521, alias No. L150, the GWR 2-6-2T making a return visit to the railway. Demonstration freight runs were made through North Weald and here the Prairie tank enters the station from the south on the Sunday afternoon.

Former LT Sentinel shunter No. DL83 was a visitor from the Nene Valley Railway for the 2022 London Transport Weekend. It operated top-and-tail with industrial 0-6-0ST *Isabel* and DMU driving motor coach 51384 as passenger accommodation on a shuttle service between North Weald and Coopersale.

The Epping Museum just outside Epping station is the only London Transport signal cabin in preservation and open to the public. Also located here since 2002 is former Acton Works yard shunter converted from 1931 tube stock cars 3080 and 3109 in 1964. In this view from 2017 it was painted white but has since been repainted yellow.

Acknowledgements and Bibliography

Thanks to Owen Hayward, Geoff Silcock and Alan Simpson for the use of their photographs.

Glover, John, *Glory Days: Metropolitan Railway* (Shepperton: Ian Allan, 1998)

Glover, John, *London's Underground*, 12th edition (Addlestone: Ian Allan, 2015)

Hardy, Brian, *London Underground Rolling Stock*, 12th edition (Harrow Weald: Capital Transport, 1990)

Jones, Robin, *Steam on the Underground* (Horncastle: Mortons, 2015)

Smith, Martin, *Steam on the Underground* (Shepperton: Ian Allan, 1995)

Programmes for *Steam on the Met*

Metropolitan Line Past and Present (DVD) (J&K Video, 2006)